Giving an Invitation for a Positive Response

Giving an Invitation for a Positive Response

Closing the Deal on a Divine Destiny

Gregory Kirby

Orman Press, Inc
Lithonia, GA

©Copyright 2006 by Gregory Kirby

ISBN: 1-891773-78-X

Scripture quotations are taken from THE HOLY BIBLE, King James version, or are the author's paraphrase of that version.

All rights reserved. No part of this publication may be reproduced, stored in a retrieval system, or transmitted in any form or by any means, electronic, mechanical, photocopying, recording, or otherwise, without the prior written permission of the copyright owner.

Printed in the United States of America

10 9 8 7 6 5 4 3 2 1

Table of Contents

Foreword VII

Acknowledgements IX

Introduction 1

Chapter One 3
The Purpose of the Invitation

Chapter Two 7
Changing Times Require An Updated Approach

Chapter Three 13
Why Appeals Fail

Chapter Four 17
Types of Appeals

Chapter Five 25
Language of The Appeal

Chapter Six 33
Alternative Invitations

GIVING AN INVITATION FOR A POSITIVE RESPONSE

CHAPTER SEVEN..37
REASONS PEOPLE SEEK

CHAPTER EIGHT..43
DESIGNING THE APPEAL

CHAPTER NINE..51
GOING FORWARD

BIBLIOGRAPHY...53

ABOUT THE AUTHOR..55
PASTOR GREGORY KIRBY

Foreword

In his book entitled, *Giving An Invitation For a Positive Response,* Pastor Gregory Kirby has provided a much-needed resource for today's churches, church leaders, and pastors. Pastor Kirby carefully gives a rational, strategic approach, and methods that can be used for persuading listeners, audiences, congregations, believers, and non-believers to make a decision. Often times, sermons are incomplete and ineffective because there is no planned appeal given to cause the listener to make a decision.

I agree with Pastor Kirby's belief that for the message to be effective, the closing invitation/appeal must be effective. I further agree that in order for a decision to be made, the invitational appeal must be planned and must flow from the body of the message. Just as the introduction, proposition and/or supposition, questions, sermon debate, expositions, and transitions of

GIVING AN INVITATION FOR A POSITIVE RESPONSE

the message are planned, so must the invitational appeal be part of the planning process.

In this powerful resource, Pastor Kirby shares his gifts, based on his formal education and his experiences. He is a much sought after lecturer and revivalist on the subject matter. He has been a guest lecturer for the past five years at a "How to Do" Ministry Fest Conference sponsored by the McCalep-Antioch-Cushite Fellowship of Churches (MACFOC), and the Greenforest Community Baptist Church, where I am blessed to be pastor. I highly recommend *Giving an Invitation for a Positive Response* to anyone, who has in the past, or plans to deliver a message in the future.

Dr. George O. McCalep, Jr.
Senior Pastor
Greenforest Community Baptist Church
Decatur, GA

Acknowledgements

I am tremendously grateful, first of all to my Heavenly Father, who called me to do this great work. He has equipped me with the talent and skills to help build His kingdom, and to train others for that most urgent work.

I am always grateful to those who work alongside me in ministry. To my friends and colleagues, thank you for your awesome encouragement, support, and even guidance. We in ministry know it gets lonely sometimes, but it's always good to have someone just a phone call away who can help us when we are in need. Some deserve special recognition, such as the Rev. Joe Gant, pastor of Calvary Baptist Church in Shreveport, Louisiana and the Rev. Leonard Leach in Dallas, Texas. The Rev. Gant has been a mentor, and in fact, gave me the foundation for the invitational appeal I use today. The Rev. Leach has been a constant friend. The Rev. Henry Lyons gave me the push I

Giving an Invitation for a Positive Response

needed, when he suggested that I write a book on appeals, after seeing my work. I am glad he recognized the potential in me. These are just a few of those who have had an impact and to whom I am grateful.

I also want to thank those on my staff who continue to work with me to do the best we can for Christ. I want to thank my sister who provided another set of eyes in the editing of this book.

Of course acknowledgments could not be complete without a special thank you to my wife, Linda, who is always there as my partner, friend, and support.

INTRODUCTION

The basic goal of ministry is to win souls for Christ. Jesus has given us all the same commission. It is simple in its command, "Go ye therefore."

The execution is a bit more difficult. Many preachers will give fiery, heartfelt sermons, and then lose ground on the appeal. Their focus is on the delivery of the sermon, not the invitation to follow Christ.

Both the sermon and the invitation deserve attention. That is because they work together. A good, strong sermon can be just the thing to attract a person to a better way of life through Christ. That sermon can prick the heart and awaken the desire for our Lord and Savior. The invitation that follows can be the impetus to get a person out of his or her seat and down the aisle, professing a new chapter in life.

GIVING AN INVITATION FOR A POSITIVE RESPONSE

Is that happening in your church? Are you consistently winning souls for Christ? Are you giving your appeal in the best way – to meet the needs of your audience? Do you vary the style, depending on the circumstance? Are you able to craft one appeal to reach a variety of people with different concerns? If not, then this book is for you.

I've been blessed to deliver some strong invitations and to have them accepted. This has not come without work and the guidance of the Holy Spirit. I have studied, trained, watched and practiced the invitation.

I want to share with you the techniques that have been effective for me, as well as answers to some common questions. This book will help fill in the gap between what you know and don't know about giving an invitation to get a positive response. We must never forget that we are to preach with a purpose expecting a positive response. We must never take this charge lightly, nor should we take for granted the opportunities we have to help someone make a decision for our Lord. Therefore, I invite you to discover how to win more souls for Christ.

Chapter One
The Purpose of the Invitation

You will find both proclamation and invitation in the evangelistic works in the book of Acts. The proclamation is where the preacher shares the Good News. The invitation is where the preacher compels hearers to respond to that Good News. We see in Scripture that many times, in the midst of this great work of proclamation and invitation, people's very hearts yearn for direction (Acts 2:37). They cry out for instruction. We can't just tell people Christ is available and think that will be enough. As Scripture states, we must explain to listeners what to expect (Acts 2:38).

When Jesus said to his disciples, "Follow me and I will make you fishers of men," in Matthew 4:19, He was painting a picture of how this work of soul winning should happen. He was giving us the great example of what we should do as fishers of men. Anyone who has ever spent time on the water bringing in

Giving an Invitation for a Positive Response

fish knows that a good fisherman not only throws out his line or net, but he also must reel in the catch. To merely throw out the line or net is just the start. So it is with a great sermon. The sermon is just the start.

The act of reeling the fish completes the action. In our work, that is the invitation. We as preachers must be the fishermen – and women – who set out to bring in the catch, or the souls. The drawing of the net is a picture of the preacher giving an invitation at the close of the sermon to bring in the unchurched, lost, sick, lame, hurting, hopeless, and helpless.

I will give you another example. Many of you may be married now, but think back to your courtship. You probably put on your nice clothes, put your best foot forward, and did nice things. As in throwing out the net, this was the first part of your work to accomplish your mission. In this case, the mission of gaining the attention and affection of the person you wanted to be your life partner. Once you did all those nice things to gain the attention, you moved to reel in. You did this by making your intentions known and letting her know what you wanted her to do. In this case, spend the rest of her life with you. At some point, she said yes. She accepted your invitation.

The early work of laying out your case warmed her up to the invitation you extended to her, asking that she marry you. So it is with our pastoral work. The early work we do in the sermon warms the listeners up to accept our invitation to join, or marry, Christ.

The Purpose of The Invitation

We extend the invitation because it closes the deal. The invitation is usually one of the least emphasized areas when it comes to church growth and the worship experience. We are anxious for people to come and hear the message but we don't put enough emphasis, thought, prayer, energy, and effort into bringing them to the point of making that divine decision. As a result, people come to our services, are challenged, then leave without really making a decision.

Chapter Two
Changing Times Require an Updated Approach

I remember when I was a boy, church was such an integral part of our lives. It was common to spend all day Sunday in service, and a big chunk of time at church on other days of the week. Life revolved around the church with its various activities; prayer meeting, choir rehearsal, and deacons' meeting. Not so anymore.

In days past, the church did well to sit back and wait for people to come to it. Children grew up in a church, then either remained members of their home churches or joined a congregation elsewhere. Today, church membership seems almost optional. This has an impact on ministry and how we view the invitation.

There were some things that were assumed in the twentieth century church and worship experience. These things were

Giving an Invitation for a Positive Response

modeled in the home and the community. Certain expectations were placed upon those who attended the worship service. That included those who were a part of the Christian community. There was a norm that was followed or adhered to, such as maintaining strong moral values and not just going to church, ultimately being involved. Those who moved into the community were seeking to quickly unite with a church. There were not a lot of preliminaries: they usually joined the church that was closest to home.

The change in today's church started basically with the maturation of the Baby Boomer generation. They were quick to get away from the norms that had ruled previous generations. These Baby Boomers were more apt to do their own thing and to reject certain social expectations. This continued with their children, especially those who grew up in the seventies and eighties.

The scale of upward mobility has played a significant role in the way people behave socially, including their church behavior. The middle class section has developed in our country as a result of the early work of labor unions, social change, technological evolution, and a greater portion of the population getting an education. We have seen more of a focus on the acquisition of things and less of a focus on church and God.

While earning more money and getting a better education are not bad things, the results have in some instances been less than good. This is especially true in ministry. When people begin focusing on their own means, are satisfied that they them-

Changing Times Require an Updated Approach

selves are the reasons they have succeeded, and that their lives are easier than prior generations, they become complacent. They see less of a need for church. They often feel that church is extraneous to their lives –that church is an "extra" and not a necessity. This very distinct middle class feels that they have more choices. This includes a choice about spirituality and church attendance.

This feeling that church is an option is a factor in our culture's decline in the spiritual and social realm. We have become dependent on a somewhat false sense of security. In many instances, it has had an impact on the family. The family is no longer anchored in a church community that can help each other through hard times and provide guidance through life's turmoil. The result is that families are making decisions about their welfare on their own, with little or no spiritual context. When families are anchored in a loving church home, they realize that they are never alone. They realize that even when things seem darkest, their Heavenly Father still looks out for them. They also realize that the fellowship and relationships they form in church can help ease their burdens. More and more families are missing this, without even realizing it. As a result, they have migrated away from church and the churches have not done an effective job of moving toward the families.

Some people are steering away from churches for other reasons, including negative preconceptions about what it means to be part of a church. Others are missing out on the church experience because today's society offers much to compete with church. Between increasing work demands, increasing entertainment choices, and uncertainty in the world, many people have put church pretty far down on their lists of priorities.

This is why we as ministers and church leaders can no longer conduct business as usual. We can't sit back and wait for people to come to us. It is imperative that we go seek them. We must make church inviting, interesting, fulfilling and essential. This includes crafting the appeal.

Our churches are dying and losing ground. We see popular anecdotes of megachurches with thousands of members, but that is not the norm. The average neighborhood church is struggling to retain old members and gain new members. Just a half century ago church going was seen as a staple in the American way of life. Now, less than half of Americans attend church regularly. Some studies put that number even less at about 20 percent.

According to a Gallup Organization report, there was a short-lived spike in attendance following the terrible Sept. 11, 2001 terrorist attacks. Many in the religious community thought the attacks would bring more people to Christ. When the shock wore off and people began to settle again into their lives, their desire for church declined.

Church growth has by far not kept pace with the population growth in America. The American people have proven their interest in spiritual matters through the increased sales of religious material. It has become big business. We see this by the number of movies and other entertainment (even games) with a

Changing Times Require an Updated Approach

spiritual slant. This presents a tremendous opportunity for those of us in ministry.

If we ignore the opportunity simply because we don't want to go out and seek those people, then we will have missed a great chance to witness. People are interested in spiritual matters. You can scarcely turn on a television set without seeing an advertisement for a movie with spiritual connotations. Spiritual themed music is increasing in popularity and so are books. With the right invitation, many of those people who are interested in spiritual matters would also be interested in a church.

I think it's a good thing that people realize they need to incorporate spirituality into their daily living. We, as spiritual leaders, have been called to help guide them along the way. The answer is a local, Bible-based church where the pastor is equipped and prepared to meet the congregation's needs.

CHAPTER THREE
WHY APPEALS FAIL

Have you ever been in a church service, experiencing a good, spirit-filled message? The Holy Spirit is moving you and the church is on fire. Whatever the case, you know the Lord is in that place.

When the time comes for the appeal, nobody walks the aisle, not a single soul. The pastor is going on and on about something. He is pulling and prodding, with some hymn such as *Just As I Am* in the background, and the soloist or choir mournfully pulling the words from somewhere deep inside.

Still, nothing works. You can see from your vantage point that perhaps there are some who would come, who may even look like they want to come, but they remain seated. Why? Often, it's because the message is unclear.

Giving an Invitation for a Positive Response

The invitational appeal must be clear. Those in the congregation are looking to the pastor or presenter making the appeal to guide them to a fitting action. You would be surprised at how many appeals fail in this aspect.

Many pastors will give earnest appeals and then go back into their office following the service, bewildered, wondering what went wrong. The problem may not have been that the Holy Spirit suddenly left. The problem may have been that the presenter didn't invite those in the pews to experience the Holy Spirit and take a stand for Christ. No matter which invitation style you choose, you must make sure you are clear and your purpose is evident. We will discuss the different styles in a later chapter.

You will have a cross section of people in your audience. From nonbelievers who have never set foot in church before, to those who once were faithful followers but somehow fell away. You can't assume that all people know what to do at this time. So tell them. You might set it up by saying something like, "I'm asking you to search your hearts and decide today to make a personal commitment to Christ."

What does that mean? You may even go on to explain that. "Step out of your seat and come forward if you want to change your life and allow Christ to lead you," or "Come down front if you are relocating to the area and want to make this your church home."

Whatever you want your listeners to do, tell them. Now is not the time to be coy, clever, or ambiguous. You must impress upon them why they must make this change. Let them know they are choosing to follow Christ because He died for them. Christ, the one who gave up his space in glory to come walk amongst men to save our souls. Christ, the only one who can save.

Let them know it doesn't cost them a thing. As long as they make a change in their hearts and take one step toward Christ, he'll meet them and walk with them. When I am giving an appeal, I often will make an offer to walk with those who are considering taking that stand. I realize that standing before a church and walking the aisle can be intimidating and incredibly difficult. I want to remove as many barriers as I can. If realizing she has an ally will help a woman choose to get out of her seat, then I am happy to be her ally. If finding out that he doesn't have to do this alone will help a man come forward, I am more than willing. Again, many appeals fail when they lack these elements: clarity, direction, and compassion.

Many people will make a decision when they are asked. They have to be asked in language they understand. Try to steer clear of church jargon that nonbelievers may not be familiar with. This is not to say you must water down the Gospel. I'm simply saying keep in mind that not everyone you come across will be familiar with certain terms. Therefore your appeal must be spoken in a language they will understand.

CHAPTER FOUR
TYPES OF APPEALS

The most common, and often used, type of appeal is "the doors of the church are open." In this appeal, the pastor, following the sermon, simply states, "The doors of the church are open". This is usually stated with a hand outstretched, as a stanza of a hymn is sung. If no one comes forward, the service moves toward the benediction and everyone is dismissed.

While that approach may meet with some success, it may not be as effective today. Considering that today's communities are different, this is another reason why I do not favor this method. It presumes the listener knows what that phrase means. Remember to be careful to use language your listeners may understand. Not everyone, especially those who have been unchurched and unsaved, will know what "the doors of the church are open" means. Therefore, the person you are trying to reach

GIVING AN INVITATION FOR A POSITIVE RESPONSE

will remain seated. In some instances, this appeal does not allow time for the working of the Holy Spirit.

As ministers, we are merely messengers, vessels through which the Lord chooses to work. When we do not make ourselves available to the appeal, we fail to allow the Spirit to maximize His use for us. Rushing through an appeal by not allowing enough time for it to penetrate a heart could be the most grievous mistake a minister can make. How would you feel if you realized that you allowed an unsaved soul to leave your service without giving his or her salvation the appropriate consideration it deserved?

Transitioning to your appeal

Once the gospel has been presented, we have to transition the hearer from a mind-set of a listener to a doer. While we are presenting the gospel, it is our expectation for them to listen. We expect them to be good listeners. In order for them to make a decision, we have to transition them.

During the transition of the appeal, we have to move them from the mind-set of a spectator to a participant. We want them to go from being listeners to doers. We want them to respond to what we are saying. We can't be abrupt and simply go from preaching to saying, "Now, get up and do this! Walk down this aisle."

The transition is designed to help put the listeners at ease, not feeling as if we are accosting them with demands. During

Types Of Appeals

the transition, you have to start with the obvious and then move toward a Biblical foundation of faith. That is why the first two or three approaches that you make should not be from the perspective of asking them to do anything. It should only engage their thinking, as you try to transition their thought pattern.

In the transition, you may begin with the practical points. You get them to think about where they are right now, not where they want to be. They are not thinking about the "shoulds" of life. They are not thinking that they "should" do this or that. The focus at this point is for them to think about their reality. We must help them realize that they are not happy with the current state of affairs in their lives, that it feels as if something is missing.

At this point, you have not asked them to do anything. You've merely helped them focus on the fact that something is wrong. You begin to talk about the goodness of the Lord and the relief that a life in Jesus can bring. It is natural for one to begin to compare and contrast the two lifestyles. You are now ready to ask your listener for something. Ask him to let Jesus lift his burdens by choosing a life in Christ. Your transition will direct them into one of several different types of appeals.

Altar Call Appeal

The appeal that we are most familiar with involves the altar call. The altar call requires the listener to make a public profession of faith. This is usually done by walking the aisle and saying why he or she has come forward to accept Christ. While the appearance of the first altar call is sometimes debated, it became popularized in the 1800s. Looked at in this context, it's a relative newcomer on the evangelical scene, but it is still supported by the Bible. We note that in the first recorded Christian sermon at Pentecost, Peter beseeched his audience in Acts 2:38 to repent and be baptized. While this wasn't the altar call we know of today, it is certainly an invitation to come to Christ.

Social appeal

In the social appeal, you are appealing to a basic desire to have an impact. In this appeal, they see that a life without Christ means they will never attain that which their hearts most crave. You may talk about things such as trying to be more productive in life or wanting to have greater influence in your community. You may touch on someone's desire to be the kind of leader the family needs or on someone's desire to improve relationships with family, friends, or a significant other. In all these cases, Jesus is the answer.

Many people live their lives for themselves and by themselves. They think all they accomplish is because of their own might. If things aren't going well, they think it's because they are not trying hard enough or working long enough. In other words, they think it's all about them and their efforts. These people have a strong desire to make these social improvements, but are frustrated because nothing seems to be happening. That is where a clear view of Jesus can help. They will ultimately choose Jesus

Types Of Appeals

because He is their Savior. Sometimes we must first remind them that He is the only way they will ever get anywhere. Once they begin to think about this, they are more likely to accept a life in him because they realize He is the Way and the Light.

Personal appeal

The personal appeal is centered on the individual's goals and achievements. In this appeal, you may have the person to think about his or her failures, finances, family structure, even current state of faith. The purpose here is to bring the person to a point where he or she looks internally, at self.

Of course every person in your audience will have a different personal life or personal concern, but you know from ministry that there are some common themes you can touch on. No matter how happy someone looks, or how successful, or even how much someone smiles, we in ministry know of the great pain that sometimes lies just beneath the surface. Talk about this pain. Draw on your experience to mention possible personal situations your listeners may be going through.

Remember, the goal in the appeal is to move the person from merely listening to you, to feeling and identifying with what you are saying. This listener ultimately draws the conclusion that coming to Christ is the way to bridge the gap. Christ will correct whatever wrong he or she finds in life. With this appeal, once you draw a picture that covers several personal situations, you go to

Giving an Invitation for a Positive Response

the Cross and let them know how laying their burdens there is the answer.

Theological appeal

The theological appeal gives the Biblical basis for the action for which you are requesting. The theological appeal relies on theological proof.

There are many scriptural references you may use, of course. A few to use are:

- "Jesus saith unto him, 'I am the way, the truth and the life: no man cometh unto the Father but by me." (John 14:6).
- "Come unto me, all ye that labor and are heavy laden, and I will give you rest." (Matthew 11:28).
- "For God so loved the world that He gave his only begotten son, that whosoever believeth in him should not perish, but have everlasting life." (John 3:16).

John 14:6 gives the unadulterated truth: Jesus is the only way to the Father. No matter what else we may believe, we know this to be true. An unchurched person, or even one who is outside of fellowship, must be informed of this. No matter how moral, how good one tries to be, or even how generous, all of that is for naught unless Jesus Christ is part of the equation. It's imperative that no appeal be completed without reminding your listeners that their very souls are at stake. It's not just about the words of the preacher, but it is about the words of our Lord and Savior, Jesus Christ.

The second passage I share is from Matthew 11:28, which is a reminder that Jesus can ease any burden. This reminder is especially effective as part of a personal appeal. For instance, as you address specific personal problems, quoting this scripture lends comfort. It reminds them that no problem is too big for Jesus to handle. If a listener is outside of fellowship and does not have a relationship with Him, this scripture can be all the assurance someone needs to at last come to Jesus.

The third scripture I share is the most powerful text that I have found to share God's love with an unbeliever or an unchurched person. "For God so loved the world, that He gave His only begotten Son…" is a declaration of God's unfailing love and care for each and every one of us. Jesus died for each and every one. Each person who hears you quote this scripture will know that Jesus died for him and that Jesus died for her.

A theological appeal gives solid support for the invitation you are laying out in front of your listeners. Used alone or in tandem with another appeal, this approach can help your listeners make the commitment they need to begin a new life.

I often use the theological appeal as the climax of my invitation. My intent is to move the listeners from a point where they are thinking of themselves and their needs to a point where they think of the great sacrifice Jesus made, and finally to a point where they think of themselves and a life with Jesus.

Giving an Invitation for a Positive Response

Often, you will use a mix of approaches in your appeal. While you may find occasions to use the theological appeal on its own, without the others, beware that using this one by itself can have the adverse effect of turning off your listeners. You don't want to beat them over the head with a bunch of scriptures that they feel is not relevant to them. That can make them feel as if you are preaching "at" them instead of ministering "to" them. I have seen many appeals go wrong in this way. A preacher will do a hell-fire and brimstone appeal, reminding all the listeners that they are sinners and hell bound if they don't repent, throwing out scriptural reference after scriptural reference. Today's listeners are constantly barraged by so many sermons on television, on the computer, in publications, and elsewhere, they have grown suspicious of sermons that try to overwhelm and persuade them by force. In delivering your appeals, remember that today's listener is a bit savvier than listeners of yesterday. They do not respond as well to appeals that use such tactics.

No matter which way you approach your appeal, remember it is a serious matter to encourage those listening to come to Jesus. The appeal is part emotion, part spiritual fact, and part faith. Even while they struggle with their decisions, it's important to remind them that the Word says that we walk by faith and not by sight. They may not understand everything the Lord is leading them to do in that moment, but that's all right. Jesus will walk with them, if they just take a step.

Chapter Five
Language of the Appeal

Each time I give an appeal, I take it as a new opportunity to be a part of someone's connection with the Lord. No matter how often we give appeals, we cannot take them for granted. The outcome can be a matter of life or death. While every appeal will be crafted for that particular occasion, there are some phrases I have found particularly effective. I will share some of these with you to help you in your own mission of helping souls see the Lord.

- "If it's right to be in church, it's wrong to be out of church." I find this to be a helpful reminder because of its simplicity. Most who attend services will acknowledge being a part of a church is a good thing. So the next conclusion is that not being a part of a good church family is not what God has for us.

GIVING AN INVITATION FOR A POSITIVE RESPONSE

- Scripture says, "Draw near to God and He will draw near to you." (James 4:8) This is effective because it lets the listener know that Jesus is right there to be a supporter, friend, counselor and anything else that is needed. Jesus doesn't ask us to shoulder the burden on our own. He is there to walk with us, and to carry us when we need it.

- "We're waiting for you." This can be the phrase to strike a personal chord with a listener. Here, we let the listener know that this moment is for him or her. A few seconds pause can give the listener who is battling indecision time to come to a conclusion about the next step. This is especially appropriate during the personal appeal, when you address a personal situation that a listener may be going through.

- "Will you trust Him?" This acknowledges that the listener may have misgivings or questions, but reminds the person that trust in God can address any of that. Many people want the assurance that God is there and that He is indeed trustworthy.

- Jesus said, "I stand at the door and knock." (Revelations 3:20) We don't want anyone to leave the church hall not knowing that Jesus is actively seeking them. We want the listeners to know Jesus has come for *them*. And they can choose to allow Him to enter their hearts. It's their choice.

These are just a few phrases you may choose to include in your own delivery. Regardless of what words you use, what tone, what music, your appeal must be sincere. You cannot just pull from your memory some phrases you've read in a book. You must let the Holy Spirit speak to you and through you. You may start with these phrases and move on from there. The appeal is a time that should flow as the Lord directs. That is why it is so important to pray on the appeal even before you enter the pulpit to speak the first word of the sermon.

Sample altar call

Here is an example of an appeal I have used. It can be adapted, and in time, you will grow comfortable in creating your own.

I know someone is here right now. You know that you need to make a choice. But you are saying, "I'll wait." Satan isn't telling you not to come; he's just telling you to do it later. But you know what? That's dangerous. One of my classmates, only 47 years old, hadn't been sick at all, missed one night at work. She didn't show up the next day for work, so her co-workers got concerned and contacted her family.

Her brother went to her home and saw her car was parked there. He knocked at the door, after receiving no answer, he broke into the house. He found his sister dead. She had been dead for two days.

Giving an Invitation for a Positive Response

What I am saying is that you can be in perfectly good health and Satan can make you believe you have time, but that is not assured. If you are not in fellowship with God, if you know you don't have the right relationship with Him, now is the time for you to make a change.

It doesn't matter what you have done in your past. It doesn't matter even what you have or what you have lost or even who you have made angry. All that matters is that you are ready for a new start.

Jesus says, "I stand at the door and knock." (Revelations 3:20) Will you let Him in? Will you accept Jesus as your Lord and Savior today? Will you believe in Him and choose to follow Him? Maybe this is your first time in church, or maybe you've been in church before but haven't been in a while. Perhaps you are new to the area or are looking for a new church home. Whatever your circumstance, whatever your reason, Jesus is here for you.

Scripture is clear, He has promised to be a friend who sticks closer than a brother. "I'll never leave you nor forsake you." God is saying, "you can trust me."

There is no failure in God. That's why the songwriter says, "O great is thy faithfulness." I know this is important to many because so often we have been let down and disappointed along the way. So it's important to know God is a faithful God. He wants us to trust Him. In fact, without faith, we cannot please Him. Perhaps you don't understand why the Spirit is leading you to make a decision, to make a commitment to the message you've heard.

But Scripture does not tell us we have to understand. God has only asked us to trust Him and have faith in Him, to walk by faith and not by sight.

It doesn't matter where you are in life. God loves you right where you are. He wants to restore you and He wants to do it right now. I am reminded of the loving father who had a son who strayed away who left the father and went to a far country. The Bible says he wasted his money on riotous living. He came to himself literally in a hog pen. He decided "I don't have to live like this. I'll go back to my father's house, and I will restore my relationship with my father and just be a servant in my father's house." (Luke 15:11–21)

This boy's father was waiting for him to come back home. God is waiting on somebody right now to just surrender and come back with a willing heart. A willing heart just to be a servant for him, just the way you are. The Bible says Jesus is waiting with outstretched arms for you to come back to the fold. Second Corinthians 6:2 says "today is the day of salvation." Not tomorrow, not next week, but today.

Tomorrow is not promised. Strange things are happening every day. This may just be your last chance.

Giving an Invitation for a Positive Response

Scripture says to us, "the day you hear my voice, harden not your hearts." (Hebrews 3:7) The old preachers used to put it like this, "While the blood is yet running warm in your veins, you need to come and make a commitment." You can give your life to Christ and make a brand new start right now.

Jesus is knocking. Will you let him in? Will you? Will you be the one? Will today be your day?

Identifying the needy

When you make your appeal, it can be tempting to call for only those who are unchurched. Depending on what you know of that congregation, you may want to design your call in a different way. We will talk more about designing your appeal in a later chapter, but here I want to help you figure out how to ascertain who is in attendance.

As you can see from the above appeal, I addressed various circumstances: the unchurched, the unsaved, and the undecided. Each church should have some kind of way to identify those in the congregation and what they seek. Perhaps your greeters or ushers will be charged with scoping out visitors and engaging them in conversation to ascertain their reasons for being in service. We take this quite seriously at our church and make certain our greeters are friendly and approachable. They are often the first people the visitors see. They are engaging, without being overbearing and polite without being stiff. We want that first contact with

Language of the Appeal

our guests to leave a positive impression. One wrong move here could turn off a visitor forever.

We know people need answers. We know they need someone to help them navigate the rough waters of life. When unsaved or people in crisis come to church, it is the minister's job to make sure they have an opportunity for relief. In our church, we work hard every Sunday, or at every service where there are seekers, to make certain they leave having made a decision of commitment. Most Sundays at Steeple, this actually happens. Whenever it does not, my heart is disturbed, and my soul is troubled. I know tomorrow or the next week is not promised. That is why we use this friendly greeter effort to help get people ready to receive the appeal. This is urgent business, as far as I am concerned.

You may find it more practical to allow your ushers or greeters to give out visitor cards to be completed. The key is to have them collected and the information conveyed to the pastor before the sermon so he or she has time to see the makeup of the congregation.

Some churches have a period early in the worship service where they invite visitors to stand and say a few words. Perhaps it is to share why they have come to your place of worship. Are they looking for a church home? Are they new to the area? While this is a way to welcome visitors, it has another use. This gives the pastor a chance to see who the visitors are and he is able to design the appeal based on the feedback he receives. I use this effective method in my own church.

Giving an Invitation for a Positive Response

When I greet visitors early in the service, it allows me to connect with them. I invite them to shake my hand after service, giving me yet another opportunity to engage them. One on one contact can never be under estimated. This method allows me to engage visitors in at least three ways in one service: allowing them to introduce themselves early in the service, speaking to their particular situation during the appeal, and chatting with them following the service. The altar call is the most effective invitation to follow Jesus that I know. Generally, a person is called to respond to the invitation by walking to the front of the church and making a public statement. In some instances, a respondent is directed to move from his seat to the back of the church. There a respondent finds a waiting counselor or prayer partner. This may be less intimidating than having the person walk to the front of the church.

Chapter Six
Alternative Invitations

The altar call requests some action on the spot. In some instances, this type of invitation may simply request the respondent to stand right where he or she is and two or three members will join the person on the spot, praying with him or her there. The altar call relies on the urgency and emotion of the moment. Some criticize it for this very reason. They say it is old fashioned or that it can intimidate people because not everyone wants to walk down an aisle in front of a bunch of strangers to accept Jesus.

I believe the altar call is one of the best invitations. However, I will share alternative means that are used by churches as they move to address a changing population. The Holy Spirit can tug on the heart in any number of circumstances; I acknowledge that some alternative methods are meeting with success.

Giving an Invitation for a Positive Response

Commitment card

Many churches, especially those with contemporary services, allow commitment cards to replace the traditional altar card. People wishing to follow Jesus simply place in the offering basket a card noting their decision. This is a non-threatening way to allow new believers to take their time in making their decision. Often joining a church by this alternative method is the result of repeated contact. In other words, the people who join by these methods tend to have visited the church over a period of weeks or months. Their decision is a result of a methodical internal process. They are not only using emotion, but also intellect when they decide to come to Jesus.

Hospitality room

Some churches invite guests to visit a hospitality room where mature Christians greet them. These members are trained to answer questions of faith, Christianity, and lifestyle. Often the pastor is present, or a member of the leadership team. Hospitality rooms are as varied as the congregations that use them, but in general, they are comfortable spaces full of smiling members serving refreshments and perhaps sharing church literature. Often, a church will provide the visitor with a small gift to take home following a stop by the hospitality room. The gift is an informational piece relating to spiritual growth, and may be a book, CD, or tape.

Alternative Invitations

Some churches invite visitors to stop by the hospitality room. They encourage the visitors to join orientation classes or to participate in some other way, even before they have accepted Christ or have become members of that congregation. The goal here is to reach out to the visitor and form a connection.

Open door invitation

Some churches simply announce the leadership's policy of being "open and available" to discuss salvation. Visitors and nonbelievers are invited to make an appointment with the pastor or to stop by the office during certain hours to talk about their lives, needs and the place Christ can have in their lives. Prospective members are able to stop by the office on their lunch breaks or on their way to or from work, have a chat and join with a membership card. This particular method certainly has convenience as an advantage.

The invitation should not be limited to what has been done traditionally. The progressive pastor or presenter will have different invitations in his or her arsenal so as to grow the Kingdom of God by multiple means. As the church changes, so can the approach, as different appeals may lend themselves to more functionality. For instance, it may not be practical in a very large congregation for all visitors to stand, give their names and their reasons for attending. A guest card may be the better choice to ascertain who is worshipping with you on this particular day. The point is to spread the Lord's Word. That's what He requires.

Chapter Seven
Reasons People Seek

The reasons people seek a church will help you design your appeal. This will help you when you decide which type of appeal to use, and even the language. Who has come to your service on this day? Why are these people there? What do they need? How will you allow the Lord to use you to meet that need?

Unsaved

The first reason for coming is the one held by those visitors who are unsaved. Unsaved is the term used for those who have not accepted Jesus as their Lord and personal savior. They are those who have not been baptized. They are not members of a church or the family of God. This is a reason to come.

Remember when we discussed not using "church jargon" in the appeal? It is important to remember that during the appeal period, the preacher must define salvation. Explain how this person's decision to give his or her life to Jesus on this day impacts salvation. It is easy to downplay salvation and to preach a "soft" gospel just to get someone to walk the aisle. However, it is important for the Bible believing preacher to make it clear that salvation is a serious thing and it shouldn't be taken lightly.

Backslider

"Backslider" was a term we heard most often in the older church. It is not used as frequently now because it has a distinctly negative connotation. Using this term can cause an uncomfortable barrier between a person wearing this label and re-connecting with the Lord.

A backslider is one who is unchurched – someone who has strayed away from the church for whatever reason. It needs to be explained to this individual the state of his condition and what is necessary for him to correct it. Oftentimes a person will feel he needs to be saved again if he has strayed away or he may feel a sense of unworthiness or guilt. The person making the appeal needs to make it very clear that being saved again or being baptized again is not necessary. It needs to be made clear that God is not mad at him and God doesn't hold anything over this person's head. The fellowship with God has been broken and communication has been distorted. It doesn't mean God loves this person any less. The person can return to fellowship with God and His church by responding to this appeal and determining to start over.

New to the area/changing fellowship

Another reason you may find newcomers attending your service is that of relocation. This may be someone who is totally new to the community. This may be someone who is interested in changing fellowship by joining a new church.

The person who is relocating needs to be recognized and identified each time the invitation is given. If you only extend the invitation to those who want to be saved or are in a backslidden state, then those relocating may not respond. Sometimes we wonder why visitors that are looking to relocate don't join or come back. The reason is that they feel they haven't been given the opportunity.

People are very timid when it comes to responding at church. While it may seem easy to get out of the seat and walk down the aisle, any little thing can deter a person from doing that. A person has to get the right cue not only from the Holy Spirit, but also from the person making the appeal.

In crisis

Many people who are saved and are regular members of a church come to service seeking relief. That particular day's message may have spoken clearly to their specific challenge or struggle. At the time of the invitation, this person may have been convicted to make some changes and oftentimes, wants to make

Giving an Invitation for a Positive Response

a public confession. So the invitation needs to include this person so he or she has the opportunity to respond accordingly.

I remember a woman who had been attending our services for quite some time. It wasn't until after a particular message that dealt with concerns that hit close to home that she responded to the invitation. She finally realized she could not shoulder her burdens alone. She chose to respond after a message that spoke directly to her. Had the appeal not included a call for those who were touched by the sermon, she may not have walked the aisle and become an active member of our church.

This is a brief description of the seekers you will find in your services. You want to include them in your invitation. Depending on the movement of the Holy Spirit, you may focus more on one type than the other.

Over and over in Scripture, Jesus acknowledges different types of seekers. He talks about those of us who are burdened and heavy laden. (Matthew 4:28) We can come unto Him because his yoke is easy and his burden light. (Matthew 11:20) He talks about those who are under pressure and stress. We can come unto him and cast our cares upon him. (1 Peter 5:7) He addresses those who know the way but for whatever reason, like the Prodigal Son, chose to go in the opposite direction, but yet return to Him. (Luke 15:11–21)

He even talks about those who have committed a grievous sin, and who, like the woman caught in adultery, may feel judged by man. (John 8:3–11) He lets even these people know that nothing shall separate a true child of God from the Father if there is repentance. Throughout Scripture Jesus presents salvation from a perspective of love, care, and compassion. He presents an invitation. He expects us to respond out of love and a desire to follow Him.

Chapter Eight
Designing the Appeal

As stated earlier, the appeal should be on the presenter's mind even before the sermon. What exactly does that mean? It means that even before you get up before the congregation, you should be thinking about the appeal you will give. You should pray about it in your study or your quiet place just as you pray about the sermon you will give. Pray to hear the Holy Spirit's direction and to meet the needs of those who have come seeking.

It's not necessary to go into the pulpit already having decided what appeal type you will use – whether you will use a social approach or a personal one, for example. You will figure this out during the service. Between finding out from your greeters, the visitors, and discerning the needs of the congregation, the appeal will come to you. You must be well versed in all types of appeals and know how to conduct them in order to deliver them effectively. Don't be afraid of the appeal.

Some pastors pray aloud immediately following the sermon and before the appeal, while others flow seamlessly from the sermon to the appeal. It is a matter of personal preference. When you design your appeal, you know that from the first word of the sermon to the last syllable of the invitation, you are on a mission.

I believe that the pastor should be the one to give the appeal, even when a guest delivers the message. The pastor is the one developing the relationship with the congregation. He is the authority figure in the church and he is the person God has placed as the shepherd of that flock. This is not a hard and fast rule. There may be instances where the Holy Spirit directs the guest minister to deliver the appeal. In some other churches, the pastor steps down after delivering a sermon. He allows the minister of evangelism or some other assistant pastor to conduct the appeal. That is permissible, but in general, the pastor of that church delivers the appeal, even if he or she is not the one preaching on a particular day.

Place of music in the appeal

Music often is the backdrop of the appeal. It certainly has been in the past. Music helped to underscore the seriousness of the moment and to also inspire an emotional response. People coming to the 21st Century church are less inclined to make emotion-inspired decisions and lean more toward logic. Music may not be used as heavily today. I believe that music is a welcome element. It should not be overwhelming and should not compete with the message of the pastor, but should complement it. Often, a soft instrumental rendition of a song or a solo is appropriate. In order to meet the needs of today's church, a pastor should try appeals both ways: with music and without.

Proximity to the congregation

Some pastors ask if appeals should be given from the pulpit or from the floor. I employ both methods, as each has its purpose. An appeal given from behind a pulpit can feel authoritative. However, an appeal given as the pastor walks the aisle can be a powerful way to connect with an audience. He is able to be physically closer to those who are struggling with a decision.

Timing the appeal

This is a question I receive often: how long should the appeal be? My answer is simple: as long as it needs to be. I've rarely seen an altar call that is entirely too long. Most preachers err on the side of making them too short. Many will open the doors of the church, glance around, maybe allow a snippet of a song, and then give the benediction.

I believe this often represents a missed opportunity. I do not believe there is a prescribed length of time an altar call should last. Each one depends on several things: size of the

Giving an Invitation for a Positive Response

congregation, number of visitors, type of appeal given, and the leading of the Holy Spirit.

I have often extended an invitation for several minutes, even 15 or 20 minutes at the urging of the Holy Spirit. I felt in my being that someone was on the verge of making a decision. Often, as I've outlined in this book, several types of appeals will be used. They are not all simply for someone to become a first-time Christian. You will also be calling for other things: you will call for those who are seeking a new church home to make a decision. You will call for those who are having personal problems to come forward for prayer. You may even call for a specific type of prayer.

I will give an example of a recent such altar call. I had preached a sermon on forgiveness. A young woman who had stood and identified herself earlier in the service as a visitor from a large ministry was touched. She rose from her seat during the appeal and walked down the aisle. Now if I had given too short of an appeal or had created a narrow focus – say, addressing only those who were unsaved – I may have missed her. As it happened, I spoke to her need in the appeal. While she was a Christian, her heart had been heavy and the altar call gave her a chance to have a breakthrough and to make a public cry for prayer as she moved closer to the Lord.

We had a very earnest prayer for her. Before that prayer, and while still extending the invitation, I let those listening know that the altar call was ending. I gave them an opportunity to come forward for their own life changing moments.

Designing The Appeal

When you let your listeners know that the altar call is ending, mean it. Don't let trickery enter here. If you say, for instance, "One last chance..." then mean it. Don't keep going on and on after you have let them know the altar call is coming to a close. Your listeners must trust what you say.

There is a thin line between inviting someone to come to Jesus and badgering. While most appeals do not go on for long enough, some go on for far too long. A minister will badger the listeners until someone steps forward. That is not appropriate nor is it God's way. We are not there to force decisions. We are there merely to preach the Word and to present the opportunity for someone to have a life changing experience, transformation or conversion.

Choosing the approach

No one approach will work in all circumstances. A minister must know the makeup of his congregation if he is to appropriately target his appeal. A congregation made up of older churchgoers may require an approach that is different from one used to appeal to the youth.

Choosing the approach isn't about which appeal type to use, but about how you will relate to your listeners. What will your vocabulary be? What will your cadence be like? Will you "hoop" or will you speak as a teacher? Just as you decide how you will approach your congregation during a sermon, you must also decide how you will approach them during the appeal.

Giving an Invitation for a Positive Response

Even the master preacher and evangelist Paul said, I am willing to become all things to all people, but even with that, he knew he would not reach all. He recognized the importance of varying your approach to fit the needs of those who seek the Lord.

Some criticize the Altar Call because they say it uses emotion or "bullying" to coerce responses. They say crafting or designing an appeal is not Biblical. I disagree. I believe any type of appeal aimed at sharing God's Word with a lost world is scripturally based. By taking the time to design your appeal shows you take this charge seriously.

Welcoming those who come forward

Designing your appeal means considering the appeal from beginning to end. We've discussed what comes before the appeal and what happens during the appeal, but we cannot forget what happens at the end of the altar call. When you allow the person who has come forward to make a statement as to his or her reason and desire, you gain valuable information. You know if this person has come for prayer, transfer of membership or some other reason. You are then equipped to address that call. You will direct the person to go with a pre-designated counselor. This is someone who is familiar with your church's operations and is a mature Christian. This person will meet with the person after he or she leaves your embrace.

The counselor should be nurturing as well as discerning. This person should be able to adequately answer the newcomer's questions, as well as facilitate the person's next steps, based on his or her needs.

There are various approaches to following up the altar call and discipling your new convert. I will advise you to consider this element carefully as this could mean the difference between helping someone begin a new life in Christ or seeing this person slide out of the doors, never to return. Discipleship involves teaching them what it means to be a Christian and finding his or her place in the ministry.

Chapter Nine
Going Forward

Now, you've designed your appeal. You've given it. You've had souls come forward. Congratulations! You have allowed the Holy Spirit to use you for God's glory. You may not have realized early on that so much time and thought went into the appeal. Once you have given it the attention it deserves, you will see responses improve.

God gives us the tools to close the deal on a divine destiny. When we use those tools, He does the rest. He moves on the hearts of men so they may be convicted.

Once the appeal has been given and completed, you'll want to follow up. I mentioned earlier the role of the counselors. I also encourage you to make contact with your new believers or others who responded to the call within 48 hours. Give them a telephone call to say hello, and to see how they are doing.

Giving an Invitation for a Positive Response

Schedule an appointment so you have more time to ascertain their needs and help them get involved in your church. Getting people to walk the aisle is the first step. Helping them grow as Christians is the next. This includes getting them involved in an orientation or new believers' class, helping them find the ministries where they can use their talents, and helping them connect with other members. We have been called to be fishers of men. Let's keep throwing out the net.

BIBLIOGRAPHY

I have consulted and learned from a wealth of resources. The following are some that have been most helpful.

    Knox, Marv. *"Will altar call go way of funeral home fans?"* Baptist Standard, May 6, 1998.

    Robinson, B.A. *"How many people go regularly to weekly religious services?"* Religious Tolerance. Nov. 26, 2001, update.

    Zaspel, Fred G. *"The Altar Call."* Word of Life Baptist Church. 1998.

About The Author
Pastor Gregory Kirby

Gregory Kirby is the organizer and pastor of Steeple Chase Baptist Church in Shreveport, Louisiana. Since 1997, Pastor Kirby has offered a caring environment and a Biblically focused, nontraditional, mission-oriented church. He attended the University of Arkansas, and graduated from Louisiana Tech University. He gained ministerial training at Southwestern Theological Seminary in Fort Worth, Texas, receiving a Master of Divinity in Church Growth and Evangelism. He is pursuing his doctoral degree with an emphasis in Church Growth and Developing Strategies for Church Planting. Pastor Kirby is sought after nationally to lecture on leadership development, church growth/evangelism, unconventional models of church planting, as well as revival preaching.

TAKE YOUR MINISTRY TO THE NEXT LEVEL

Do you want more examples of strong invitational appeals? If you want even more training in the art of the effective appeal, visit www.gkirby.org, or call (318) 686-8600. Let Pastor Gregory Kirby train your staff in this important area of ministry.

Experience Pastor Kirby's appeals

CDs and DVDs of Pastor Gregory Kirby's appeals also are available. Listen to Pastor Kirby give a strong delivery. Learn how to modulate your own tonal inflections. Learn how to effectively use music, pauses, and speech to achieve your goal. Visit www.gkirby.org to order.

It's coming!

Pastor Kirby is already at work on his next book. This exciting title on church growth will give you innovative strate-

GIVING AN INVITATION FOR A POSITIVE RESPONSE

gies to increase your membership. Learn what works and what doesn't. Gain insight from Pastor Kirby's own experience as well as what he has discovered in his extensive study on the topic. As the pastor of a relatively new church, he has seen tremendous growth. Let him give you new ideas to keep interest high and to take your congregation where it needs to go. Pre-order now at www.gkirby.org or by calling (318) 686-8600.

www.ingramcontent.com/pod-product-compliance
Lightning Source LLC
LaVergne TN
LVHW041458070426
835507LV00009B/660